# Songwriting 101

Inspiration, Tips, Tricks, and Lessons for the Beginner, Intermediate, and Advanced Songwriter

$2^{nd}$ Edition

Rake Helson

## Legal Notice:

This Book is copyright protected. This is only for personal use. You cannot amend, distribute, sell, use, quote or paraphrase any part or the content within this Book without the consent of the author or copyright owner. Legal action will be pursued if this is breached.

## Disclaimer Notice:

Please note the information contained within this document is for educational and entertainment purposes only. Every attempt has been made to provide accurate, up to date and reliable complete information. No warranties of any kind are expressed or implied. Readers acknowledge that the author is not engaging in the rendering of legal, financial, medical or professional advice.

By reading this document, the reader agrees that under no circumstances are we responsible for any losses, direct or indirect, which are incurred as a result of the use of information contained within this document, including, but not limited to, —errors, omissions, or inaccuracies.

# Table of Contents

# Introduction

I want to thank you and congratulate you for buying the book, *"Songwriting 101: Inspiration, Tips, Tricks, and Lessons for the Beginner, Intermediate, and Advanced Songwriter"*.

This book contains proven steps and strategies on how to write songs whether you are a beginner, intermediate or an advanced songwriter.

Writing a song is a challenging task, and not everyone is born with this talent. But even if you do not have inherent songwriting skills, you can still learn how to write songs that many people can relate to. You do not have to be a professional lyricist who has attended workshops on songwriting. Just make sure that you follow the tips written in this book if you want to get started in the craft of songwriting. When you do, you will find that your mind becomes very aware of the songs around you, of how rhythms and beats work and will also be able to use the experience of listening to recognize which qualities are those which listeners really want to be incorporated into song.

With so many styles of music available in this day and age, there is room for everyone to try their hand at songwriting. The most amazing songs come from the most unexpected of circumstances and whether you are writing for a special event or just because you want to share your songs with others, motivation plays a huge part in songwriting and helps you to find the words that work with the tune so that the whole song is a showcase of your skills.

Some of the greatest songwriters of our times have been poets such as Bob Dylan, and his roots lay in the old protest songs, which gave him the impetus he needed to put his thoughts into words. Whatever your impetus comes from, grasp it when it happens and become a songwriter that uses conviction and belief in the power of words to capture the hearts of your audience. It's satisfying, and it's fun and anyone can do it though only those who know the tricks of the business do it well! This book is written for everyone from a vast experience of songwriting in all kinds of genres.

Thanks again for downloading this book, I hope you enjoy it!

Rake

# Finding Inspiration

Songwriting can be difficult if you do not know where to begin. You need to start somewhere before you can string together words and sentences and make great lyrics. The first thing that you need to do when writing a song is to find inspiration. Your inspiration is anything that stimulates your mind to do something, like writing a song. For songwriting, your inspiration is that single idea which your song will revolve around. Here are some tips on how to find inspiration for writing songs. Many experienced songwriters have used the same formula, and it works because it draws on personal thoughts, experiences and observation of life.

## Use your own experiences

You can get ideas for a song from your own experiences. You can write about your childhood, your first love, your first heartbreak, your experiences as a parent, your marriage, your relationship with your parents, and so on. You can also write about something that is not too personal like your experience when you go to the beach or when you attend concerts. A lot of artists use their own life experiences when writing songs. You do not necessarily need to name names or make it specific. You can simply use general ideas from your experience when writing a song. For example, Paul McCartney wrote the song *Hey Jude* for John Lennon's son named Julian as a way to comfort the boy when his parents split up. Notice how he used the name *Jude* instead of *Julian?* You can also do the same thing if you are going to write about personal experiences. You can also write a song about bad experiences. In fact, people who have had bad experiences are the ones who can write great songs because pain inspires more creativity than happiness.

There are many examples of how songwriters have incorporated life experiences within their songs, and some stories are very sad ones indeed. For example, Eric Clapton wrote a very astute and heart-rending song called "Tears in Heaven" in tribute to his son that died young. The words are very clever but say a lot of the things that people think about when death happens. For example, he incorporated the notion that his son may not recognize him when he gets old and dies and goes to heaven. No matter what your experience, and whether it's sad of celebratory, it's a good place to start with songs because writing about something you know is always going to be easier than trying to force words from situations you are unfamiliar with. For example, not knowing much about the rap community, without having experienced it firsthand, I would not try to attempt to write rap. It takes experience of all kinds of different stimuli to actually get a song written about it. As a professional songwriter, sometimes I am asked to write songs out of my areas of experience. The way that I do that is simple. I experience whatever it is that I am supposed to write about first. Then I write the song. Experience is everything.

## Read books, watch movies

You can also write lyrics about stories that you have read or watched. These stories should make a huge impact on you for you to be able to write lyrics about them. One popular song based on a book is David Bowie's song titled 1984 which was based on George Orwell's dystopian novel *Nineteen Eighty-Four*. The rock band *Deep Blue Something* sang a song called *Breakfast at Tiffany's,* which is about a man whose girlfriend is planning to break up with him. He reminded his girlfriend that they both like the movie, which starred Audrey Hepburn, and that is one thing that they have in common. If you are going to depict popular media such as movies, characters from TV or anything of this nature, know your subject. Don't just take a brief look and think that's enough. An in-depth study always helps because the words flow much more naturally when you are aware of the subject that you are writing about.

## Write about people

You can also write songs about people who have been a part your life like your boyfriend or girlfriend, spouse, best friend, parents, sibling, grandparents, and so on. You can also write about groups of people in general like people who live in your area, soldiers, teachers, and homeless people. You can also find inspiration from famous people like musicians, authors, artists, politicians, and celebrities. There are a lot of famous songs about people like Don McLean's *Vincent,* which is about the post-impressionist painter Vincent Van Gogh or Elton John's *Candle in the Wind* who was originally written for Marilyn Monroe but was later on rewritten for Princess Diana.

The point is that writing about people gives you an instant picture in your mind of what that person has done in life or what they stand for. That in turn gives you words and that's what you are looking for. The French singer, Pascal Obispo, wrote a wonderful song as a tribute to his child being born and it took all the elements of new parenthood into the picture and spoke of the wonder of the smallness and fragility of the child.

## Listen to a lot of music

If you want to be a great songwriter, you need to listen to a lot of songs for you to have an idea how famous songwriters do it. You need to know the different styles for you to develop a style of your own. However, be sure to develop your own style instead of copying the style of another songwriter because you want people to recognize your own style. Rephrasing lyrics is a big no-no unless you want to be branded as a copy-cat. Just use other people's lyrics and music as an inspiration and as your guide to writing your own songs. Listening opens up your mind to styles, but when you go to write your own songs, these use your own chords, melodies, and words. How listening helps is that it means that you have a better idea of what's acceptable and what is not and that gives you guidelines to work within, which is essential for great songwriting.

## Write about your passion and interests

If you are passionate about something, you will find it easier to write lyrics about it. For example, if you are passionate about the environment or about politics, you can make songs about these topics. You can also write about going to the beach or going to parties. You can write about anything as long as you use your heart when writing. For wonderful examples of passionate writing look at the works of Joan Baez during the sixties as these were really passionate works about what was happening politically at the time. There are hundreds of singers who did that and whose work has passed the test of time because it made part of history. If you can get hold of the DVD on Woodstock and listen to the songs, you will see how these were writers that took political situations they felt strongly about and put them into the lyrics of the songs that they produced. Perhaps your passion today is conservation or global warming. Perhaps it doesn't run that far and is more inclined toward parties and fun. It doesn't matter what that passion is. Within your passion, and only you know what that is, lies a whole wealth of material that you can use for songwriting.

## Listen to your feelings

Songs that come from the heart are the best ones because the listeners feel like they are taking a glimpse at the songwriter's personal life. Moreover, people who listen to heartfelt songs can relate because they have experienced the same feeling at one point in their life or another. You can write about your current love interest, your loneliness when being away with your loved ones, or your feelings of grief when someone you love passed away. Emotions are strong and are universally accepted as being great material for songs. The Bodyguard movie showed a powerful song, sung by the late Whitney Houston, which showed the power of love. "I will always love you" was sung with such a lot of emotion that it was unforgettable. If you are going to write powerful songs, you also need to think about the voice that will deliver them and the range and tone of their voice because the delivery of the song is vital to the success the song will glean.

## Do crazy things and use your imagination

If you want to have something interesting to write about, you should consider trying some crazy things. You should start living a colorful life full of things that you can write about in your songs. If you are a homebody who does not go out or experience a lot of things, you will have fewer ideas to write about. If you go out and try fun and crazy stuff, you can tell people all about it, like living in a bus that travels the whole country or sailing in the Caribbean. Well, perhaps these ideas are a little off the wall, but you need experiences to relate to, and some crazy ideas have come from the imagination of great writers. How about Octopus's Garden from the Beatles? They don't come much more way out than that, and although this wasn't about real life, it used great imagination for a fun song idea. If you can't get out and about, it doesn't stop your imagination from exploring and using its thought processes to produce imaginative songs.

## Travel to different places

When you leave the house and visit different places, you can learn a lot of things, meet a lot of people with different backgrounds, experience different cultures, and taste different cuisines. The people who travel have a lot of things to tell if they want to write a story or a song. One popular song related to traveling or vacation is *Surfin' USA* by the Beach Boys, which talks about the different surfing spots in the USA. Now look at the songs of Bob Marley and you instantly think of Jamaica. There is a whole world out there to explore and the more you take in, the more materials your mind has to put into song.

## Choose random ideas

If you really cannot think of anything to write about or if you want to challenge yourself, you can pick a random idea by writing down several topics and putting them in a box or hat before picking one. To make it even more fun and challenging, you can ask your family and friends to come up with at least two ideas each and add them to your box or hat as well. This will challenge even the most advanced songwriter because you never know what you will get. You might pick up something as random as 'pineapple' or something difficult like 'biology'. Good luck in coming up with lyrics about these topics. Lyrics are all about putting words together to rhythms, and good songwriters can usually come up with something regardless of how "out there" the idea appears to be. The incorporation of a word into a song, an idea into a song or even an emotion into a song is what songwriting is all about.

## Write about your daily life

You can also write about what is happening in your daily life. You might say that you have a boring life and writing a song about it will just bore your listeners out of their skull. That is the challenge in writing songs about your daily life. You need to write it in such a way that will make your life seem interesting. This is where your creativity comes in. There was a very creative singer-songwriter in the sixties called Gilbert O'Sullivan and if you have never heard him sing, then it may be worth listening to a couple of the songs he wrote because these were taken from everyday experience of life. For example "Nothing Rhymes" typified his life in the northern part of the UK and encompassed ideas from that simple life. You may think that your life isn't that interesting, but your perspective of that life always will be. Somewhere in the world there is someone who sees life very different to you but who is open minded enough to want to hear what you have to say.

These are just pulling a lot of ideas out of the hat to give you a little intro to where songs come from. You may find that your lifetime has a whole load of episodes that are worthwhile writing about. You may find that people around you or who have inspired you are worth using in songs, and certainly beliefs and ideologies are things that help you to find the words to fit the rhythms of songs, which you can be proud to put your name to.

# Who Provides the Music?

The songs that you write have to fit into music. That means that you need a little understanding of how music works. In music, there are phrases or sections, just like in a poem and these have a fixed length of time or number of beats attached to them. I personally write lyrics for other people, but also play guitar and my guitar work helps me in writing songs. However, in this day and age of technology, I also write lyrics for people across the globe who ask for them and who provide me with the background music to listen to and who give me ideas of the theme of an album so that my ideology when starting to write the song is on the same wavelength as theirs.

For those who are writing their own songs with music, you will need to create a melody but sometimes it helps to have a little bit of the lyrics in order to write the song. Sometimes you come up with ideas and it's always a good idea to have a notebook so that you can jot these down. Ideas are fleeting. If you don't remember them, then the chances are that the idea has gone forever. The Beatles came up with a song called Penny Lane, originally started by Paul McCartney about an area that he knew from his youth. Stuck for ideas, John Lennon's input was sought and together, the two of them came up with words by talking about their childhood in Liverpool and remembering certain elements of that childhood. This is a great way to collaborate with other musicians on the words of a song though this may appear to be going off topic a little. The thing is that the song you write has to have a melody, but the memories that you have of the place will dictate the kind of music that you are going to produce. In the case of Penny Lane, it was an upbeat song about a place that figured greatly in the past of members of the Beatles. It wasn't a sad time. It was a time when the boys were out discovering who they were. Thus, the upbeat melody that they chose was very suitable and fitted with other tracks on that same album. You need to decide the tempo, the style and the kind of tune your song should be played to so knowing the content of the song a little intimately helps.

Sad songs – Melancholic songs would have a fairly slow beat and if you are experienced at using the guitar, then A minor is a good chord to strum to get a feeling for the sadness of the song.

Happy, joyful songs – Try strumming G, D, and C, etc. until you find the beat that suits the kind of song. This isn't giving you the words at this stage. It's just giving you a rhythm to work with.

Melancholy but memorable songs would use a B7. That's a beautiful chord and is used in songs such as "Hallelujah" in the version sung by Rufus Wainwright.

The point is that you need a feel for a song. If you are starting from scratch, playing a few chords at differing speeds or even picking to those chords or playing them on a piano or keyboard can give you inspiration. This in turn helps you to create your lyrics and then you can perfect your musical arrangement to your song.

If you are working with the music of someone else who has asked you to provide lyrics, then this is a whole different ballgame. You need to find out the ideas that the artist of the music has because if you don't have the same mindset as them, you may find yourself writing a love song when in fact what he wants is a heavy metal song. Collaborations are great fun, and I collaborate with people as far away as Dubai whose culture is totally different from my own. By talking with the musician who has produced the music, I get a better idea of how to fit my lyrics into their ideology, and that's vital.

There was a musician in Boston that once contacted me for lyrics of a spiritual nature but when speaking to the guy, he hadn't let on that the work should also have a Celtic twist to it. You need to know these things because they are all important to the words that you produce. It's not enough to listen to their music. Their ideology and the ideas that they have about the production of that music and what genre it is aimed at is also vital to your songwriting.

This chapter is really about who is going to provide the music. If you are doing your own, then you also have a good idea of whether the song is going to be sad or happy and the kind of genre that you want to write to. If it is to be someone else that provides the music, then you need to have this in advance, so that your songwriting is made easier by knowing what the musical style is and what the musician expects you to produce to fit in with other songs that he may have in mind for the same album. Albums are generally themed and thus if he already has the music and words for other tracks and knows the style, this helps you to produce consistent work which will fit in with what the musician has in mind.

Perhaps they have favorite artists that they want you to listen to. If you are unfamiliar with the style of music, take the musicians favorites and use these as a guide because if they really are favorites, then the kind of music he is expecting you to provide will fall in with that same kind of genre and you'd be pretty safe trying to come up with something that's in that ilk.

# Fitting Your Words to Other People's Music

Having been commissioned for a lot of songwriting gigs, I have developed methods which work both for the provider of the music and for me. A songwriter needs to absorb the music and listen to it several times before they are able to write the words needed. It's very much a mood thing. There are ways that a musician can help with this, and this is called using the Lah Lah method. In effect, you are asking them to provide you with the background music that they intend to use but for them to use the words "Lah Lah" to represent where they want the words to be sung.

Musical composition is very complex. A piece of music may give you the impression that your words have to fit the whole piece of music that has been sent to you when quite often a musician wants musical freedom between verses or has ideas about the way that the words fit into the scheme of things. The music itself may give you an idea of the theme or the overall background of a song, but the lah lah gives you even more clues as to the length of each line of the verses. It's a very easy overlay for a musician to add to a track before they send it to you and if you don't have this layer, ask for it because it makes your songwriting much easier.

Deciding on the length of verses and where the chorus comes in is pretty simple. Where you find repetition in the lah lah rendition, you can pinpoint these areas as chorus, but remember that chorus – although the words may vary a little from chorus to chorus – is not the main theme of the song, but may be important enough to need the punch line.

An example of this is the song Hallelujah written by Leonard Cohen. The verses were very deep and meaningful, and each chorus was a repetition of the main theme of the song, which was indeed Hallelujah. The more that you listen to music, the more you will understand the purpose of the chorus and YouTube is a great place to listen to similar genres so that you also get a feel for the type of words, the harshness of the words or the subtlety of them in that particular genre. When asked to write punk music, I wasn't even sure what was considered as Punk and a visit to YouTube was able to give me a very clear picture of what it was and how Punk music used chorus. The same can be done for any genre of music so don't be scared to listen and learn because if you do, you are much more likely to write a song that hits the right market.

## Writing down the beats

This is always a fun part, but you need to be in a quiet place to do this, where you have no interruptions. You also need to have a piece of paper and a pen or pencil because what you are going to be doing is listening to the music provided, with the Lah Lah included and you need to note on the paper the lah lah's that occur so that you know how many syllables you can get away with in that particular line of music. It takes a while to get used to doing this and you may need to go back to the start when you lose track. Write down one stroke of the pen for each Lah and when you feel that the phrase is finished, move onto the next line and do that. This gives you a clear picture of the verse formation and the chorus formation. You get to know instinctively after a while which part of the lah lah forms the verses and which is the chorus.

Turn the music off at the end and then count up all the lines you drew for each line of the music. This tells you how many syllables you can get away with for that particular line. Syllables are only an indicator and, as in poetry, some words flow better than others. As you begin to write your song, read it out loud because sometimes a change of word here and there makes it flow better, and it's the flow that really matters when it's going to be sung.

Revise, revise and revise again. It's vital that you play the music and that you sing the song with it to see if the words that you have written fit perfectly with the background music that you have been provided with. Before sending the words back to the musician who produced the music, verify that all of your words are the best choices and sound good. You can record it if you have the potential to record because this tells you if the words need alteration. Sometimes when you listen to a song after recording it, it's instinctive that a word is out of place and your best chance of acceptance of the song that you wrote for the musician is when the words fall comfortably into place with the music, without any unnecessary pauses or words that don't sit right.

Always remember there are copyright issues with writing lyrics. If you are going to write lyrics, agree on the terms before you produce them. If you want your name credited to the lyrics, get this in writing as once you produce the lyrics, the musician may not have in mind to give you the credit you deserve for providing the words to fit his music. I always insist on this and get it in writing before producing the work and passing it to a client. If you want to build your reputation as a songwriter, then every success should clearly be shared with you by giving you credit on the album for producing the words. Similarly, you can ask for credit on any website where the music is shared with others, such as YouTube, MySpace, etc. because it is your reputation as a songwriter that is on the line.

# Writing the Lyrics of Your Own Songs

Once you have settled on an idea that you want to write about, you can now start writing the lyrics. Some say that songwriting is a spontaneous activity that does not have a formula. However, if this is not working for you because you are not feeling spontaneous right now, you should consider following some easy steps for songwriting. You can use the guide below when writing a song about a specific topic that you have chosen.

## 1.   Be focused

The first thing that you need to do is to focus your lyrics on your chosen topic. If you focus your lyrics on one general idea, it will be easier to write the lines because you have a single idea to work on. Focusing your lyrics means saying what you have to say to your listeners without extra lines that do not contribute to the whole meaning of the song. When talking to someone, you want the person to not beat around the bush and just be straightforward. Although there are lyrics whose story builds up as the song nears its end, each line is coherent and leads toward the main idea of the song.

For example, if you are writing a song about love, you want it to be focused on this emotion alone. You can include other emotions like anger, pain, or jealousy but make sure that the underlying theme still points towards love.

To create song lines about a specific idea, you should come up with words or phrases that you associate with the main idea. Going back to the previous example, if your main idea is 'love', you can write related words and phrases like 'my spouse,' 'happiness,' 'marriage,' 'two hearts become one,' 'promise,' 'walking hand in hand,' 'grow old together,' 'through thick and thin,' and many more. By looking at the words and phrases that you have written, you can write about the love between two people who have been married for many years.

## 2.   Be creative

When writing song lyrics, you have to be creative especially if you are going to write about a cliché topic like unrequited love or missing someone. You need to know how to write your lyrics in a unique and creative way that will set it apart from all other songs that have a similar topic. Your listeners may be hooked to your song mainly because of how real the lyrics are, but creativity in your song is a nice touch. However, you need to avoid being overly creative or your lyrics will sound pretentious. You do not need to write poetry with highfalutin words and expressions to be labeled as creative. You can still use ordinary words, but you need to find a way to say it creatively.

One good example of a creatively written song is *I Miss You* by the band Incubus. The topic itself is a cliché because a lot of songs have been written about missing someone. What sets it apart is the creativity of the lyrics, like the line *'I see your picture I smell your skin on the empty pillow next to mine'* is another way of saying that you are missing someone.

You can also use rhyming to make your song more creative. If you have a difficult time coming up with lines that rhyme, you need to develop a strategy that can help you write rhyming lyrics. For example, if your lines goes like *'I wandered along the empty road,'* you can make a list of words that rhyme with 'road' like load, ode, owed, bestowed, glowed, snowed, mode, goad, flowed, and so on. Your lines do not necessarily need to rhyme but songs that rhyme are easier to remember so you might want to try it.

## 3.   Be casual

You should also write in a casual way as if you are talking to a friend. Writing poetry allows you to be formal by using formal words and expressions. Writing songs is different because you need to write using casual words if you want to reach out to your listeners. Like what was mentioned earlier, writing highfalutin words will only make you sound pretentious and trying too hard to be creative. You need to stick to words that your listeners can relate to because you want your listeners to imagine themselves in the lyrics of the song.

For example, instead of writing 'I fabricate stories' you can say 'I make up stories' which is more casual and familiar to your listeners. The trick here is to write from your heart and write as if you are writing to a friend or someone you know. You need to write to express and not to impress.

## 4. Repeat words and nonsense syllables

Another step that you should try is to repeat words or syllables in a song. The repetition in a song hooks the listeners to listen to the song. Some popular examples of songs with repetition are Foo Fighter's *Best of You* where the phrase 'the best' is repeated several times. Kylie Minogue's *Can't Get You Out of My Head* also repeats the syllables 'nanana' a number of times throughout the song. Repetition makes the lyrics of these songs catchy and easier to remember.

## 5. Understand the melodies

Although this book focuses on writing the lyrics, it wouldn't hurt to know the basics of melodies. The melody should complement what is being said in the lyrics. For example, if one verse of the song sounds angry because the speaker in the song has been cheated on, the melody should also sound angry. There may be changes in emotions throughout the song, and it is important that the melody or music also changes depending on the lyrics. However, there are some songs that have angry lyrics but soft melody. This is also a great way to write a song, but you have to choose the right kind of soft melody for it to work.

Sometimes, melodies are uniform all throughout the song. However, it is more common to find songs that have changing melodies especially those songs that have the standard verse, chorus, and bridge format. A song becomes more interesting if there are repeating elements in the song, like the verse and chorus melody in a song. The bridge melody is the element that does not get repeated, which gives the song a breath of fresh air because of its uniqueness.

The verse melody should not give anything away about how the song will unfold to keep the listeners tuned in. It is like the background of the song's narrative before the important parts of the story or the climax happens. The chorus melody gives the listeners a kind of conclusion to the song. This is where the lyrics unfold the main idea. Both the lyrics and the melody need to be conclusive. The bridge verse has a unique melody and is used as a tool for emotional outpouring. These are the basic melodies of a song. There are other melodies that can be included but be sure to start with the basics first, especially if you are a beginner.

## 6.   Think of a great title

Another important tip is to come up with a great title that can be easily remembered by your listeners. You can come up with a great title after writing the song or before writing the song. This depends on which comes first to mind. One advantage of having a title in mind before you write the song is that it guides you on what lyrics to write. On the other hand, coming up with the title once you have written the song and incorporated the music gives you enough leeway in your lyrics. Some titles are related to the song while others are not related at all, although the songwriter has a personal reason for choosing the song title.

## 7. Understand your genre

You also need to understand your genre to be able to write the right kinds of songs. There is really no strict format, but certain styles are more acceptable in certain genres. For instance, when writing pop songs, you can use words or phrases repetitively so that people will be able to sing to them easily. The meaning of pop songs should also be straightforward, like songs by Britney Spears or Justin Bieber. On the other hand, rock music like music produced by Coldplay or Nirvana usually has a deeper meaning. Country music often tells stories of love and heartbreak while hip-hop usually focuses on money, sex, and bling. Of course, these are generalizations, and you can find songs that are different from other songs in their genre. But it would be best to follow what's popular in your genre especially if you are a beginner.

## Tips when writing a song

If you are going to sit down and write a song using the guideline above, you should be in a quiet and relaxing place where you can be in your own thoughts without any distraction. If you can work easily while playing your musical instrument, then go ahead and use your musical instrument. You need to have a pen and paper ready or your laptop ready to write down the lyrics that you have come up with while brainstorming. Do not discard lines that you think are not good right away because you might be able to use them later on. It is also a great idea to bring a pen and a small notebook with you wherever you go where you can write down your ideas that pop into your head spontaneously. Your mind should also be in good condition if you want to concentrate on writing. If you have a lot of worries like bills and chores, it will be difficult to focus on the task at hand because your mind will wander to the other things that you should be doing.

# Writing Down Ideas

Songwriting means having an accumulation of ideas and putting them together to go with a tune. Some people like to work both tune and words at the same time. I like this particular idea because I can sing out the words as I write them and make alterations if I don't think they sound right. This also gives me a chance to play around with the tempo and the choice of chords for the long, as well as the picking patterns that work with them.

## Writing down potential lyrics

Sometimes you come up with ideas for song lines during the course of your day. Grab these words because if they are as spontaneous as they obviously were when they occurred to you, they may be just as catchy for a song. People often think that songs have to have lyrics that rhyme just like poetry does, but this isn't necessarily the case. Songs are more about sounds. Let's have a look at a famous song and dissect it so that you see the different elements:

"She'll be coming round the mountain when she comes."

Okay, the writer has chosen a 4/4 beat and thus the writer couldn't have changed the words at the end because it wouldn't have gone in with that beat. Let's demonstrate how that beat works. It's a case of counting as you go through the words.

In this case, the first beat doesn't come in until you get to the emphasized word "coming."

| 1 | 2 | 3 | 4 |
|---|---|---|---|

She'll be coming round the mountain when she comes

So why is the last 4 off the end of the line? This is because the music that is played behind the words goes on to finish the phrase. The chosen number of syllables is important but so is the order of the syllables. Let's try a variation and you see what I mean.

She's be coming round the mountain when it's summer

This version doesn't work because you would have to cram the words "its" and "summer" together to get it to fit into the music created in the background. It has too many syllables or sounds, and it's clumsy. The impact of the original song is much better cut off with the word "comes."

They go on to repeat the same line twice, add an extended line in the middle and then go back to the original line, which is a perfectly acceptable format for a song. What you will notice is that it's not like rhyming poetry. Repetition is used rather than rhyme, and that's common in songwriting.

## Exercise in songwriting

This is an exercise in trying to rewrite a song. It's not to use the same tune. It's not to use the same words.

The only thing that is the same is the theme. It's about the mountains. It's about someone arriving. Apart from that – you are free to use your own creative juices except that it should take on the same beat as the original song. I am going to do this too as it's not a theme that I have ever written about, and it's an interesting exercise in timing.

Tap your foot with each of the beats as shown above the words in the outline of the old popular song. Don't tap fast. Tap with where they appear in the song. Tap, Tap, Tap, Tap. This gives you a speed to work with for your particular song line. Okay here's my attempt and this is written completely spontaneously.

He'll be back by the time the clock says ten.

And here are the foot taps that go with it:

|   1   |   2   |   3   |   4   |
|-------|-------|-------|-------|

He'll be back by the time the clock says ten.

Then you can go on and add enough sentences to it to make a verse. In my case this could be,

He'll be back by the time the clock says ten,

And I never thought I'd see his face again.

Note that the words "again" and "ten" do not rhyme, but they have a very similar sound so work well together. The idea is to build up an entire verse. If you have a powerful leading line to your song, listen to it in your head, add to it and listen, add more and listen. Knock out all the extra sounds that you don't want. Change a word if it has too many sounds. Stretch a word within the song to give it more sounds. People do this all the time. What you are aiming at is writing a verse and singing it. Then you can work on the chorus.

The more ideas you write down, the more you can look at those ideas when inspiration strikes and build upon the songs that you are trying to produce. Some of my original songs took months to perfect while others were spontaneous and very quick to produce. It's really a matter of grabbing words from thin air that you think would sound catchy in a song and then sitting down to work with those words.

I am pretty much at the stage of my writing career where people can throw an idea at me and I can instantly come up with a tune and a verse but it takes a little more time to get the whole song and it's worth going over it and going over it again, listening to it in the form of a recording and being aware of which words don't fit correctly. Simon and Garfunkel have a knack for songwriting, and the harmony of their songs is so good. While these may be simple listening, the writers will have gone through the same process as I am describing, putting their words together on paper and building up the whole repertoire of a song to include the following elements:

- Opening line
- Chords to be used
- Number of verses
- Choruses

Whether the song needs more than simple backing

The last item relates to whether more parts are needed in the music such as other instruments or orchestral backing and this is important when you write song words, because you are building up a vision of what it is that you are creating.

There is a very clever example I can give you here when it comes to musical composition. When Mark Knopfler wanted to pay a tribute to a guitar maker, he actually used themes from the emails of the guitar maker as part of the music. This song was produced following the purchase of a guitar and Mark wanted the song to mark the event. He produced a video of the song and the music chosen was soft guitar in places and then built up into a crescendo with orchestral music that brought the whole song together. It worked as a powerful example of how words, background, and intention as well as subject all helped the music to become a whole entity.

If you are aiming your lyrics at professional agencies, for example, they need to see your idea and if you think music should be added to it you can note this on your musical score and let the agency decide upon the arrangement of the music.

The writing down of ideas is what's important. The reason I mentioned the Mark Knopfler story more than anything else was this shows perfectly how things around us influence us and give us ideas for songs. In his case, the words of the emails or perhaps the sign off of the emails came to mind as they would be cryptic comments like "the chisels are calling..." which meant that the guitar maker needed to get back to work. In your life, there can be little hints of potential songs at any time. If Mark Knopfler had simply replied or deleted the emails, the ideas might never have come to him. Similarly, if you dismiss moments when ideas come, the chances are that you never get them back again in the same intuitive way. This, always carry a notepad, even if it's a small pocket-sized one, and be sure to make notes of words that mean something to the writing of your next song.

Songwriting is a skill that can be learned by anyone and whether you are currently a musician or not, if you can write down words and express feelings or emotions in words, you may find you have it in you to be a songwriter. However, if you don't write down the ideas as they happen, you are missing opportunities, and that's a huge mistake. People are still looking at the writing of old songs for inspiration. They turn to see how established artists went through the process of songwriting because this also helps them to get ideas put into songs. Be inspired by others, but be original to your own ideas and thoughts because all of the notes that you take of words that cross your mind as potential for songs help you in your final writing process.

# Influences and the Importance of Listening

If you were to ask one the greatest songwriters of our time what their early influences were, you would find that they are able to tell you straight away who that influence was. Bob Dylan, for example, obviously took his inspiration from Woody Guthrie. Don McLean would readily admit that his influences were a cross between Buddy Holly and Frank Sinatra – both of whom are at different ends of the musical spectrum. You could go on forever looking at who influenced who, but there would always be someone that they held up as being an example of musical talent they respected. On the other hand, musicians and songwriters such as Joni Mitchell found that her influences lay in the classics such as Stravinsky and Chopin. I often wondered about the influences that a songwriter as individual as Joni Mitchell would have used as ideals, but in fact this lady broke the songwriter mold by breaking the rules, producing great songs with very deep meaning, but using melodies that were a little harder and deeper to understand than classic rock. Perhaps it was her classical influences that affected her approach.

In general a music writer will use the music that they are accustomed to and that give them inspiration to also give them ideas for their own songs. These can be diverse, but the wider the range of songs you are influenced by, the more individual your work is likely to be. Listen to songs a lot and try to take in more than just superficial listening. Words written by other songwriters may influence you but may also show you the direction in which your musical talents should go. Listen for the following elements when you are using other artists for inspiration:

- Which artists fall into the genre you want to write?

- Which have the range of notes you are comfortable with listening to?

- What kind of beats are you aiming at?

- What age of audience do you want to target?

These are all important considerations when you go to write a song. In the old days of the sixties, most of the young were hungry for being part of the hippy culture. This culture used music as a means of expressing themselves. It wasn't just about entertainment. It was about breaking away from taking part in wars that seemed to have no purpose. It was about not following in the footsteps of parents whose lives seemed to be so constrained by society's expectations. The songs of Dylan, Joan Baez and many of the artists of this time were all focused on a kind of audience, a kind of empathy for them and a kind of solidarity that people could feel comfortable with. This is why the songs lasted the length of time that they did. They may have been a culture shock at the time, but they represented the people, and good folk style songs should uphold what people are thinking during the times that they were written. They are a history of a country or region and as such it was easy for singers to use these for influence when writing songs.

However, nowadays, with so much technology out there, you need to be switched on to the type of people you want to listen to your songs and the audience is much more diverse. Thus, listening on a regular basis is your education as a songwriter and an obligation to some extent because it teaches you so much about the way that songs are put together, the popularity of certain types of song and the target audience that songs such as yours should be marketed toward.

It's not as simple as sitting with a guitar and writing a tune anymore. If you really want to make it big time as a songwriter, all of this background information will help you to decide which direction your music is going in so that the words come much more easily and are not confused by not actually fitting into any specific genre.

If you have an iPod, listen to as wide a scope of music as you can. Listen to the emphasis of words and how words fit into the music because this is all an education in songwriting from people who are successful and who are on the music scene right now. A particularly good example of a songwriter who has kept up with what's happening on the music scene is a singer who calls himself Passenger. This balladeer has managed to accumulate sufficient wealth from his songwriting through standing on street corners as a street musician to finance his own albums. The words of his songs are nostalgic and well written, but this proves the incentive to listen to others. He learned what was popular. He fitted his kind of music into an existing market gap and gained success from doing this. As for his songwriting, that stands out on its own. True to himself, his choice of style and using clever lyrics to capture his audience, he really has done well and that's just someone like you or me who decided to put all of his energies into what he believed was the right road for him. There are thousands of examples of singer-songwriters who you can listen to and who can influence the way that you approach your songwriting career.

# Lessons on Songwriting

You need to know some useful lessons that will help you write song lyrics successfully. Whether you are a beginner, an intermediate or an advanced songwriter, you can use these techniques for writing songs.

## Do not be a perfectionist

You might be disappointed in your first few attempts to write a song. This is normal because you are not perfect, and you cannot write a perfect song that will become a hit single after your first try. It takes practice and patience to master songwriting. The most important thing here is to not give up when your songs did not turn out as you have expected. You need to just keep on trying even after you have made mistakes. As they say, practice makes perfect. Or at least practice makes great songs. The other thing is that you may just be trying to find your feet in the musical business and may not have found your perfect genre yet.

If you think of great musical stars of today, some of their songs were disappointing, but as they progressed their songs got better, and their style developed into what you now recognize as their style. It didn't happen overnight but was an evolutionary process. Expect the same evolutionary process to happen to you. Artists such as James Blunt hit the scene with an absolutely outstanding first album that was very hard to live up to in future albums because there was so much work that went into the first album and a lot of energy as well. You need to find a pace that works for you and your music. Don't expect it all to happen overnight, and never think your work is so good it cannot improve. There is always room for improvement and being a perfectionist will actually get in the way of your creativity.

## Songs and poems are two different things

Some people who write great poems think that they can use their poems as lyrics to a great song. This does not exactly work like that. Although poems and lyrics have things in common such as rhymes, rhythm, and cadence, you need to remember that lyrics are meant to be sung. This means that you should avoid using words that are difficult to pronounce. Songs also have a wider audience than poems so be sure that your lyrics are easily relatable. It's more than that. It's a difference of presentation.

Whereas a poem adheres to a set format, the format of songs is only dictated by the musical composition. Words don't have to rhyme, and more emphasis is placed on sounds and how words sound in the context of the song. Yes, some poets make first class musicians as well but you don't have to be a poet to be a songwriter. Those who are, such as Bob Dylan use their talent in being able to pass a message through song. Since the songs were written as songs, rather than poems, he already knew the rules about sounds and used them to his advantage. To give you some idea of what is meant by poetry and songs being different, pick up a poetry book and try to sing one of the poems and you'll instantly see that it doesn't work like that. The sounds of the words sung are so much different than when the words are simply spoken.

## Get feedback

In anything that you do, getting feedback is important because feedback lets you know what you need to improve and what you should continue doing. By getting feedback, you will become a better songwriter because it teaches you to hone your skills more until you receive positive feedback. You can show what you have written to your family and friends, or you can perform the song in front of an audience. You need to ask for their feedback and their suggestions on how to improve the song. If you know someone who is a seasoned songwriter, you can get professional tips from him for you to improve your craft. If you receive negative feedback, do not be discouraged because this is normal especially in the entertainment industry. Instead, you should use these criticisms to grow as an artist and as an individual.

## Consider collaborating with someone

When it comes to songwriting, two heads are also better than one. If you collaborate with someone in writing lyrics to a song, you will have more ideas about what to write because you have different strengths, weaknesses, and experiences. You can work together for some great ideas for a song, and you can use each of your strength to collaborate. If you are good at translating your thoughts and feelings into words, you can work with someone who has a knack for creating catchy melodies. I mentioned in an early chapter about collaborations when a songwriter is working for a client, but there is no reason why this cannot work with other songwriters to help the words flow. Great artists do this sometimes, and groups such as the Beatles are no exception. Many of the songs were collaborations between Lennon and McCartney and other groups have followed that same winning style of sharing ideas.

## Develop your own style

Although you can get inspiration from other songwriters, you need to develop your own unique style in writing songs early on. You want people to recognize your songs as your own even before they see your name on it. This is something that you should strive for even if you just started to write songs. This will also depend upon the musical background that you choose and who sings it, as the voice is very important. For example, Passenger had a very vulnerable but clear voice, which went well with the songs that he was singing. The more familiar you are with different artists and their work, the more you can see how personalization of your works is vital to getting known as a songwriter. Another thing to remember is that if you don't have the talent to sing, it doesn't stop you being able to write songs. Others can sing the songs that you produce, but it's important to have your trademark on the songs so always take credit as a songwriter for the songs that you produce.

## Enroll in a songwriting class

If you think you need the help of a professional or someone who can really write songs, you should consider enrolling in a songwriting class. There are songwriting classes offered at music schools and local universities, and you can enroll in these classes during your free time. There are also songwriting lessons that you can find online. You can watch videos or read manuals on songwriting. Another way to move forward without having your songwriting influenced too much by a taught style is to actually take up learning an instrument. For example, I switched from piano to guitar simply because of the logistics of my home but when I did, that introduction to guitar was first rate for helping me to develop my skills as a songwriter. If you take this course, do be aware that learning a new instrument is time-consuming, but it's worth the energy put into it because it makes your songwriting much easier to do. For example, in the past, I may have to play the piano, write down the notes and then add the words, but with the guitar and a notepad I can try different rhythms with words and see which fit best and adjust words as I play to fit the chosen guitar rhythm.

## Schedule a time for songwriting

If you are serious about songwriting, you need to set aside time every day to practice writing songs. You can set aside an hour a day if you have a regular job or if you are a student. If you have a regular schedule for writing songs, it is easier to hone your skills and become a great songwriter. Songwriting requires commitment and consistency. Besides, if you love to write songs, finding time to do it should not be difficult to do. In scheduling your time for songwriting, what is fun is scheduling online meetings via Skype with collaborators or arranging to get together with like-minded musicians even if it's in your garage because musicians and creative people inspire others, and that brings the best out in your songwriting. You may even find that one of your friends, who has never tried songwriting, would enjoy collaboration with you and that you work well together. Many collaborations between musicians are spontaneous but work out to be very successful, one musician making up for the lack of inspiration of the other, keeping the amount of work they are able to turn out consistent.

## Look at the bigger picture

Instead of analyzing the bits and pieces of your song, you should consider analyzing it as a whole to see which element does not work. The reason behind this is that one detail may seem like a great idea but not when you incorporate it with the other elements. You need to listen to your song carefully and ask yourself if something is still missing. Maybe it needs to be more energetic, or maybe the lyrics lack power.  By looking at the bigger picture, you will be able to easily pinpoint what needs to improve to make the song better. Playback is always important when you write songs, and often I play mine and see how the words flow, making adjustments when I think of words that would work better than the original ones that I have chosen. Sometimes, you need to distance yourself from the song for a while and then go back to it. Play it through and record it even if you use a fairly primitive form of recording on your computer and then really listen to what it is that your song's message gives to a potential audience. I do this all the time and also am not afraid to ask for feedback from close friends. Those who care about your musical career won't mind listening and giving you ideas of which part of the song looks like it needs a bit of extra work. In retrospect, I usually agree with them. It's always helpful to get feedback, and you should never be put off by what you see as negative feedback.

## Songwriting is not all about talent

Just like in any skills that you want to develop, writing lyrics to a song requires a lot more than innate talent. Being a talented songwriter is not enough to produce really great songs that listeners will love. You also need to have patience, diligence, and perseverance. You should keep on practicing and improving even if you know that you have raw talent in songwriting. Compare it to a person who has raw talent in playing tennis. He may show potential but if he does not do something about it, he will not develop into a great tennis player. I remember songs that I produced in the early days of my songwriting career that I thought were great at the time. Now, when I listen, I sometimes wish I had taken more time and that I had used different lyrics because with a few tweaks, those songs could have been greater. The point is that all the practice in the world will never make you perfect. If you think that you are perfect, you are likely to stop trying, and that's when you really become stale. Think of one hit wonders and that's exactly what happens when you give up trying to please your audience.

Even the Beatles and the Stones used an evolutionary process to stay at the top of their profession. If they hadn't have done that, they would have lost popularity years ago. The Beatles, split up and working separately, went on to produce some great songs but instead of being specifically written for a group of four, they were solos, or written for newly formed groups and some of these are very memorable indeed although taking on a new style. John Lennon, for example, moved over from Merseyside pop to more serious works of a solo nature. McCarthy formed Wings and the music produced was totally different from that of the Beatles. George Harrison moved forward into a more mystical and meaningful type of music that he is remembered for today. If they had stagnated, they would probably be less well known than they are now. Each of the musicians mentioned had talent, but they would be the first to say the same thing. If you don't have talent, then practice at what it is that you want to do, and you'll get better at it in the same evolutionary process that they used to become popular.

## Use technology

Songwriters today are lucky because they can use technology to make their jobs easier. Some purists may think that using technology in art whether it is painting or songwriting diminishes the art's greatness. This is not exactly true; an art is an art whether you use technology or not as long as you employ your own creativity and skills. When composing songs, you can use music composition software that allows you to organize your work and listen to what you have finished. This makes the task of arranging your music and incorporating lyrics to music a lot easier. You may want to incorporate beats. You may play pieces of the music and use overlapping to make the sound stronger. Technology doesn't create the music for you. Technology uses your ideas to create the songs, and that's a subtle difference.

If you can get a recording program that's half decent, that's also very useful. I tended to use recording programs on my iPad, but there are a whole lot of apps that you can use to help with the mixing of songs. Mine were based on instrumental background so didn't need too much mixing but there are still going to be areas of a song where the background needs to be softened in order to let the song break through or vice versa. Software may be something that you want to play with between writing sessions. It may provide you with ideas that you can use in your writing, but far from taking away creativity, it helps you to produce near perfect sound recordings which may even help you to sell the songs once they are finished.

## There is no wrong or right in songwriting

Songwriting is a form of art that can be used to express your thoughts and emotions. It is not an exact science where there are right and wrong answers. In songwriting, you can write anything you want without being labeled as right or wrong. However, songs can be labeled good or bad depending on different factors such as the quality of music and lyrics and the preferences of the listeners. The way to judge your music is to ask yourself what the audience is getting from it. It's a form of release for people who want to tell others how they feel but perhaps can't find the words. In a documentary that I watched recently,

Steve Moakler said that what was neat about his music was that audiences actually listened to his songs and nodded their heads in total agreement giving him the heads up that they were totally in the same groove as him when it came to being able to say in music what he meant and that's what good songwriting is all about. No, there are no wrongs when it comes to songwriting, but by goodness, when you get that reaction, there's something very right that feels good inside. Work toward releasing all those inner feelings of turmoil that fit the style of song and you achieve that and it feels amazing.

## Learning to use past emotions for future songs

There is always going to be an upside to negative emotions. They help you to grow spiritually and also help you to have a lot of resources you can dip into at any time during your songwriting career. I remember painful things from the past, and I can actually recall how much they hurt and how deep that hurt was. I don't tend to relive them in songs, but I do tend to look back on those emotions and use them as fuel for new songs to fit various events in my life. For example, asked to write a song as a memorial for someone that had died, I was able to grasp the sadness from my past and translate this into a song that was suitable somber and sincere so that it suited the occasion, but also so that it left a mark of respect for those people who had lost a family member. It's hard writing songs for personal events such as this, but I have been faced with this many times and dipping into your emotions or your past negative experiences helps you to translate that into song words that are super sincere and heart felt so that your songs really do hit home to listeners seeking a little bit of hope.

Look at artists like Janis Ian and you find that songs that hit home are those that really do hit vulnerable spots within your very soul, and that's what songwriters try and capture. In her song "Seventeen" she told the story about how kids that didn't measure up to society standards felt about their lives and how society expects everyone to be perfect when, in fact, this is far from reality. I listened to that song twenty years ago, and I listened to it again yesterday and it evoked the same feelings within me. When a song can do that it helps greatly to get an audience that want more of your songs. They are raw, they are real and they are true to feelings that people feel but seldom get a chance to express.

## How songwriting can be liberating

Imagine who you are and who people actually see when they look at you. People have set ideas about what's right and what's wrong and, in fact, it's not often that they can live up to the ideals of society. People do foolish things. They make mistakes, but they don't tell folks about those mistakes because it would make them look extremely foolish. You date a married man, but you don't broadcast it to the world when he doesn't leave his wife like he promised to. What happens when you put these kinds of emotions into song is that you liberate yourself, you learn to forgive yourself but you are also helping thousands of potential listeners who know what that feeling feels like but have no one to share it with. Songwriting really is liberating. It allows you to say what you feel without anyone actually knowing that these songs are about you, your experiences and your dramas. In song, they are acceptable. Use the dramas within your life to trigger words that really do stick in the minds of listeners. You will be amazed at how many listeners will buy your work based on the fact that it is honest and it is raw and up close and personal to the emotions that people closet rather than share with others.

## Using Mood to enhance your writing skills

A lot of fellow songwriters agree with me that the mood you set when you write songs matters. Whether you do your song on paper or whether you use new technology doesn't matter as much as the mood you create it in. For example, sitting and strumming the guitar can often give you clues as to the depth of your feelings right at any given time. If I'm upbeat, then my strumming will be as well. It could be anything from the beat of a Samba through to a liberating song of the sixties style, but your mood will always dictate the kind of song that you are writing. Thus, when I need to write sad songs, such as those described above for a memorial, I need to be in a serious frame of mind. That comes fairly easily with music because you can switch your listening to change your mood. You certainly wouldn't listen to the Spice Girls and then go and try and write a song about loss. The genres clash. However, there's nothing wrong with setting the mood by listening to the kind of music you want to produce. One of my personal favorites is a very personal song of Don McLean called "Empty Chairs" as this puts me in the frame of mind I need to be in for sad songs. I play this one regularly because it's a reminder of how transient life is and how fleeting moments are.

When I have created the mood for the type of song I have to create, I tend to play around with the guitar and starting with that A minor which is always sad, I strum and change chords randomly until I find a melody that kind of fits the occasion or the style of music. You could say that if everyone wrote songs in this way, there'd be a lot of repetition of the same chords being used but in actual fact there already is. If you look at websites such as Chordie and gaze through some of the songbooks, you will find that many of the songs use the same chords in different sequences, but what makes those songs written by individual artists so independent of each other is the way in which the music is played. You have different tempos, you have different rhythms and you have different words and all of these combine into a song and although the chords used may commonly be used in other songs, the way you use them and the words that you sing will be different and will be yours.

Strumming leads me to all kinds of melodies, which in turn inspire me into writing words, and that's where songs come from. They come from putting yourself in the mood, getting a nice melody going and then adding part of you to it that wasn't there before.

## Using belief to get your creative juices working

Sometimes you hit a stumbling block along the way, and the words don't flow that well, particularly when you are in the initial stages of learning. This happened to me several times and the advice that I am about to give you worked for me. I found that I was too flippant, too distant from what I was writing about. Perhaps I didn't have enough feeling about the subject matter of the song or was too distant from what the music producer was asking me to provide him with. At times like this, which are a little similar to writer's block, what I tended to do was look at the genre of song. Then look at how I personally felt about situations and particularly look at really negative or happy thoughts depending upon what I was supposed to be producing. How can you produce sad songs when you are infinitely happy? How you can produce sincerity within your words if you are not in that space where the song is supposed to be coming from? I found the answer for me was to put myself in that space through personal memories. Let me give you an example.

One producer asked me to write a song about destruction. Not being a particularly destructive person, it was hard to get my head around the concept. Sure, there are words that you can use to represent destruction but words aren't enough. You have to feel the sentiment when you write songs, particularly if you want them to stand out as being good songs. What I did, in this case, was meditate for a while to clear my mind and then tried to remember a time in my life when I was destructive. We all have those memories stacked up somewhere for occasions such as this. My particularly destructive behavior was aimed toward a sibling, but it didn't matter what the action was. All I needed to grasp from it was the destruction and anger that I felt at the moment of the act and by putting myself back to that time, I could do that very easily.

Using this as the basis for setting the mood, it was a lot easier to actually write the song and to put more than just words into it. That feeling of desolation and of personal betrayal that led me to destruction came out as a clear message in the song and the music publisher emailed me back to tell me that it had hit the spot and that he didn't believe that someone as mild as me could have come up with such powerful lyrics.

By the same token, I would use mood to help me in all the following genres:

- Love betrayal
- Deep love
- Happiness sharing
- Sadness
- Loss
- Portraying images

As I was writing this and thinking back to the type of songs that I had written, I suddenly realized that the last item was as important as the mood setting ones because in one song, I needed it to be relevant to a certain place and time when friends were getting married on a beach. They had chosen this particular part of the world because of the tranquility and the nearness that they felt to their God in that place. It had been a place that had figures largely in their meeting in the first place since they had gone there for a retreat, looking for spiritual fulfillment and the song had to reflect everything about that place, the picture of the couple on the beach and also the picture of the couple's original visit to that place when they were searching for hope in a world that had given them nothing short of disappointment. This was a sequential song and songs have to be sometimes. This helps you to get the storytelling into action within the words of the song.

In this case, I started with a very melodic but sad way using words that described the search that both of them had gone on to discover something better than they had yet experienced, but I needed to describe the beach, the meeting of minds or souls, the warmth gleaned from each other. It was a bit like painting a picture but before I could paint it, I needed so much detail from the couple and they may have thought me a little obsessive at first. The image that they gave me, with begrudged information about their lives, helped me to word the song in a way that was personal to them and which was so meaningful to the guests as well.

When you are writing songs such as this, you can use the natural flows of sadness and quiet, building up to a crescendo as if life has thrown out possibilities and reflects the waves on the shore, which bring about change. That was the main theme of the song, like the old tide had washed away the tears and hopelessness and that the new tide had brought about a certain peacefulness and calm that the couple were able to share.

If you have a very vivid picture in your mind, you can paint beautiful pictures with words and that's what good songwriting is all about. There are songs I remember hearing and thinking how they had painted pictures of a moment in time so astutely, and I mimicked that kind of nostalgia that works. Think about the song "Unforgettable" and the words are amazing and even rock bands occasionally knock you out with words such as the words of "I don't want to miss a thing" by Aerosmith seem inspired words that stay in your mind and that make songs into more than just words. Look at the songs sung by Ava Cassidy and some of those are amazingly beautiful and capture the essence of the moment magnificently. You too can do that, but you have to be in the right space in your mind to do that.

## Not being afraid to experiment

Many commercial pop songs that don't go beyond being a one-minute wonder are lost because they don't hold meaning for listeners. Others hit the right spot at the right moment. People are not that good at expressing what they feel sometimes, and songs allow that expression without people pointing at you and considering you pathetic for thinking in that way. Don't be afraid of expressing feelings and of being different from the norm because when you do, you will find that the voice inside of you is able to come up with words that really hit the mark. Before you experiment with different types of songs ask yourself:

- The purpose of the song
- The occasion it needs to fit
- The age group of the intended audience

Soak up ideas that hit all of these criteria before you take pen to paper. Listen to what's out there and do better. Never imitate. By all means, be inspired, but you don't have to compete by imitating what others are doing. Make your own songs hit the mark by being different to what is being offered, but equally as valid.

## Try something different

Just because you have to pick a genre or a specific style for your songs does not mean that you have to be stuck writing the same kinds of lyrics again and again. You want people to recognize your songs because of your unique style and not because all your songs start to sound the same. You can change the way you write lyrics a bit to make your songs more interesting and to catch your listeners off guard. For example, if you always write sad love songs, you should consider writing about female empowerment, which is a far cry from what your listeners are used to. This will give your songs a variety which will surprise your listeners in a good way.

There are writers of ballads that have produced great beats as well. For example, writers such as

Don McLean managed to write all about music in American Pie and then switched tempo to very nostalgic songs all on the same album. If you can do that, you can be sure of attracting an audience that will be ever eager to see what your new songs are like. However, there are also those who try too hard to change their style out of self-indulgence and miss the mark. Audiences know them for a certain style and love that style. Don't make the mistake of jumping too much from one style to another until you have more confidence in your ability to supply words for different kinds of music. You may end up regretting that change. It's a matter of easing yourself into new styles, listening to different music and being able to make your own interpretation of styles that you become familiar with.

It's a very gradual process but one that can work exceptionally well for versatile songwriters who open themselves up to working for different groups or music producers, rather than writing songs to sing themselves. I write my songs for music producers rather than for me to sing unless these are for special occasions such as weddings or memorials where a single voice is enough and the songs are personal the participants in the event.

The best tip that I can give you on songwriting is to let your mind have more freedom than it has in everyday life because sometimes intuition gives you some wonderful words to express your meaning and people all over the world may just be thinking the same thing but are afraid to say it. Bob Dylan and many of the writers of the sixties voiced the opinion of their generation. Others use songs as a more personal thing to express feelings, but people can enjoy these just as much because personal feelings affect every human being who listens to them. They may be songs that will be listened to for comfort, for nostalgia or simply for knowing another human being felt the same as they do at a particular time in their lives. Whatever you write, let your creative voice speak and don't second guess it. Often the original words you thought of are every bit as good if not better than the ones you put on the final draft. I once turned one of my songs back to the original draft and compared it. The original was the best and written in exactly the right mood to produce a great melody.

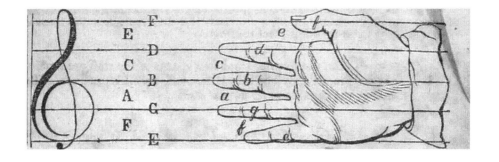

# Conclusion

Thank you again for buying this book!

I hope this book was able to help you to learn effective tips for writing songs whether you are a beginner, intermediate or advanced.

The next step is to use what you have learned in this book when you start to write songs.

Finally, if you enjoyed this book, please take the time to share your thoughts and post a review on Amazon. It would be greatly appreciated!

Thank you and good luck!

— Rake

# Other Books To Check Out

**Songwriting–Crafting A Tune: A Step By Step Guide To Songwriting**

http://www.amazon.com/dp/B00UA8C226

# Photo Credits

Made in the USA
Lexington, KY
26 December 2015